Rnd 3: Working in back lps, ch 3, dc in same st as beg ch-3, 2 dc in each rem st around, join in 3rd ch of beg ch-3. *(40 dc)*

Rnd 4: Working in back lps, ch 3, dc in same st as beg ch-3, dc in each of next 3 sts, [2 dc in next st, dc in each of next 3 sts] around, join in 3rd ch of beg ch-3. *(50 dc)*

Rnd 5: Working in back lps, ch 3, dc in same st as beg ch-3, dc in each of next 4 sts, [2 dc in next st, dc in each of next 4 sts] around, join in 3rd ch of beg ch-3. *(60 dc)*

Rnd 6: Working in back lps, ch 3, dc in same st as beg ch-3, dc in each of next 5 sts, [2 dc in next st, dc in each of next 5 sts] around, join in 3rd ch of beg ch-3. *(70 dc)*

Rnd 7: Working in back lps, ch 3, dc in same st as beg ch-3, dc in each of next 34 sts, 2 dc in next st, dc in each of next 34 sts, join in 3rd ch of beg ch-3. *(72 dc)*

Rnd 8: Ch 3, working through both lps, dc in next dc, *ch 3, sk next 3 dc, (sc, ch 3, sc) in next dc, ch 3, sk next 3 dc**, dc in each of next 2 dc, rep from * around, ending last rep at **, join in 3rd ch of beg ch-3. *(16 dc, 24 ch-3 sps)*

Rnd 9: Ch 3, dc in next dc, *ch 2, sk next ch-3 sp, (**3-dc cl** *(see Special Stitches)*, ch 3, 3-dc cl, ch 3, 3-dc cl) in ch-3 sp between sc *(flower made)*, ch 2, sk next ch-3 sp**, dc in each of next 2 dc, rep from * around, ending last rep at **, join in 3rd ch of beg ch-3. *(8 flowers)*

Rnd 10: Ch 3, dc in next dc, *ch 5, sk next 3-dc cl, sc in next 3-dc cl, sk next 3-dc cl, ch 5**, dc in each of next 2 dc, rep from * around, ending last rep at **, join in 3rd ch of beg ch-3.

Rnd 11: Ch 3, dc in next dc, *ch 3, **V-st** *(see Special Stitches)* in next sc, ch 3**, dc in each of next 2 dc, rep from * around, ending last rep at **, join in 3rd ch of beg ch-3.

Rnd 12: Ch 3, dc in next dc, *3 dc in next ch-3 sp, sk next dc, dc in ch-1 sp of next V-st, sk next dc,

3 dc in next ch-3 sp**, dc in each of next 2 dc, rep from * around, ending last rep at **, join in 3rd ch of beg ch-3.

Rnd 13: Ch 3, dc in each dc around, join in 3rd ch of beg ch-3.

Brim
Rnd 14: Ch 3 *(does not count as first dc)*, **fpdc** *(see Stitch Guide)* around beg ch-3 directly below, **bpdc** *(see Stitch Guide)* around next dc, [fpdc around next dc, bpdc around next dc] around, join in first fpdc.

Rnd 15: Ch 3, [fpdc around next fpdc, bpdc around next bpdc] around, join in first fpdc.

Rnds 16–20: Rep rnd 15. At end of last rep, fasten off.

Medium
Rnds 1–6: Rep rnds 1–6 of Small. *(70 dc)*

Rnd 7: Ch 3, dc in each of next 3 dc, [2 dc in next dc, dc in each of next 5 dc] 11 times, join in 3rd ch of beg ch-3. *(81 dc)*

Rnd 8: Rep rnd 8 of Small. *(18 dc, 27 ch-3 sps)*

Rnd 9: Rep rnd 9 of Small. *(9 flowers)*

Rnds 10–13: Rep rnds 10–13 of Small.

Brim
Rnd 14: Rep rnd 14 of Small.

Rnds 15–21: Rep rnd 15 of Small.

Large
Rnds 1–6: Rep rnds 1–6 of Small. *(70 dc)*

Rnd 7: Ch 3, dc in same st as beg ch-3, dc in each of next 6 dc, [2 dc in next dc, dc in each of next 6 dc] around, join in 3rd ch of beg ch-3. *(80 dc)*

Rnd 8: Ch 3, dc in same st as beg ch-3, dc in each of next 7 dc, [2 dc in next dc, dc in each of next 7 dc] around, join in 3rd ch of beg ch-3. *(90 dc)*

Rnd 9: Rep rnd 8 of Small. *(20 dc, 30 ch-3 sps)*

Rnd 10: Rep rnd 9 of Small. *(10 flowers)*

Rnds 11–14: Rep rnds 10–13 of Small.

Brim

Rnd 15: Rep rnd 14 of Small.

Rnds 16–22: Rep rnd 15 of Small.

Scarf

Row 1: Ch 27, dc in 3rd ch from hook *(beg 2 sk chs count as a dc)*, dc in each rem ch across, turn. *(26 dc)*

Row 2: Ch 2 *(see Pattern Notes)*, dc in each dc across, turn.

Row 3: Ch 2, dc in each of next 3 dc, ch 3, sk next 3 dc, **V-st** *(see Special Stitches)* in next dc, ch 3, sk next 3 sts, dc in each of next 2 dc, ch 4, sk next 4 dc, (sc, ch 3, sc) in next dc, ch 4, sk next 4 dc, dc in each of next 4 dc, turn. *(1 V-st, 10 dc, 2 sc, 2 ch-4 sps, 3 ch-3 sps)*

Row 4: Ch 2, dc in each of next 3 dc, ch 2, sk next ch-4 sp, (**3-dc cl**—*see Special Stitches*, ch 3, 3-dc cl, ch 3, 3-dc cl) in next ch-3 sp *(flower made)*, ch 2, sk next ch-4 sp, dc in each of next 2 dc, ch 4, sk next ch-3 sp, (sc, ch 3, sc) in ch-1 sp of next V-st, ch 4, sk next ch-3 sp, dc in each of next 4 dc, turn. *(1 3-dc cl, 10 dc, 2 sc, 2 ch-4 sps, 1 ch-3 sp, 2 ch-2 sps)*

Row 5: Ch 2, dc in each of next 3 dc, ch 2, sk next ch-4 sp, (3-dc cl, ch 3, 3-dc cl, ch 3, 3-dc cl) in next ch-3 sp *(flower made)*, 3-dc cl in same sp, ch 2, sk next ch-4 sp, dc in each of next 2 dc, ch 5, sk next 3-dc cl, sc in next 3-dc cl, sk next 3-dc cl, ch 5, dc in each of next 4 dc, turn. *(1 3-dc cl, 10 dc, 1 sc, 2 ch-5 sps, 2 ch-2 sps)*

Row 6: Ch 2, dc in each of next 3 dc, ch 3, sk next ch-5 sp, V-st in next sc, ch 3, sk next ch-5 sp, dc in each of next 2 dc, ch 5, sk next 3-dc cl, sc in top of next 3-dc cl, sk next 3-dc cl, ch 5, dc in each of next 4 dc, turn. *(1 V-st, 10 dc, 1 sc, 2 ch-5 sps, 2 ch-3 sps)*

Row 7: Ch 2, dc in each of next 3 dc, ch 3, sk next ch-5 sp, V-st in next sc, ch 3, sk next ch-5 sp, dc in each of next 2 dc, ch 4, sk next ch-3 sp, (sc, ch 3, sc) in ch-1 sp of next V-st, ch 4, sk next ch-3 sp, dc in

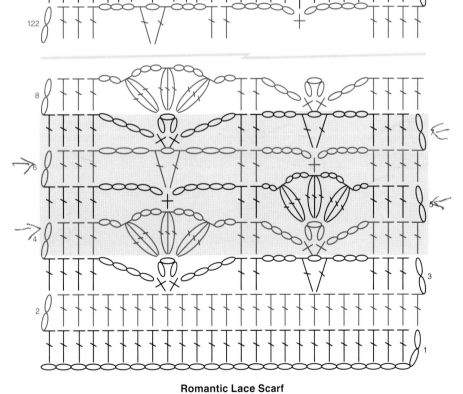

Romantic Lace Scarf
Stitch Diagram
***Note:** Reps shown in gray.*

each of next 4 dc, turn. *(1 V-st, 10 dc, 2 sc, 2 ch-4 sps, 3 ch-3 sps)*

Rows 8–119: [Rep rows 4–7 consecutively] 28 times.

Rows 120–122: Rep rows 4–6.

Row 123: Ch 2, dc in each of next 3 dc, 4 dc in next ch-5 sp, dc in next sc, 4 dc in next ch-5 sp, dc in each of next 2 dc, 3 dc in next ch-3 sp, dc in ch-1 sp of next V-st, 3 dc in next ch-3 sp, dc in each of next 4 dc, turn. *(26 dc)*

Row 124: Ch 2, dc in each dc across. Fasten off. ●

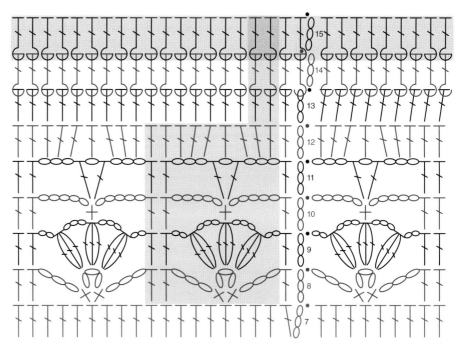

Romantic Lace Hat
Stitch Diagram Rnds 7–15
Note: *Reps shown in gray.*

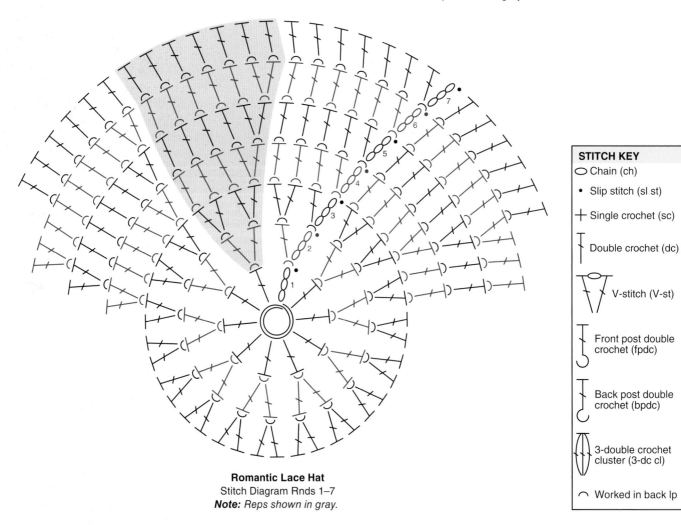

Romantic Lace Hat
Stitch Diagram Rnds 1–7
Note: *Reps shown in gray.*

STITCH KEY

◯ Chain (ch)

• Slip stitch (sl st)

+ Single crochet (sc)

† Double crochet (dc)

⋁ V-stitch (V-st)

Front post double crochet (fpdc)

Back post double crochet (bpdc)

3-double crochet cluster (3-dc cl)

⌢ Worked in back lp

Man's Hat & Scarf

Designs by Lisa Gentry

Skill Level

 EASY

Finished Measurements

Hat: 8 inches long x 22 inches in circumference

Scarf: Approximately 5¾ inches wide x 66 inches long

Materials

- Red Heart Soft Yarn medium (worsted) weight acrylic yarn (5 oz/256 yds/141g per skein):
    2 skeins #4614 black
    1 skein #1882 toast
- Size I/9/5.5mm crochet hook or size needed to obtain gauge
- Tapestry needle

Gauge

Hat in pattern: 15 sts = 4 inches; 11 rnds = 4 inches

Scarf: 15 sts = 4 inches; 11 rnds = 4 inches

Pattern Notes

Refer to Stitch Diagrams as needed.

Weave in loose ends as work progresses.

Join with slip stitch as indicated unless otherwise stated.

Chain-3 at beginning of round or row counts as a double crochet unless otherwise stated.

Chain-2 at beginning of round or row counts as first half double crochet unless otherwise stated.

Hat

Rnd 1 (RS): Beg at top and with black, ch 4, **join** *(see Pattern Notes)* in first ch to form ring, **ch 3** *(see Pattern Notes)*, 11 dc in ring, join in 3rd ch of beg ch-3. *(12 dc)*

Rnd 2: Ch 1, 2 sc in same ch as beg ch-1, 2 sc in each rem dc around, join in beg sc. *(24 sc)*

Rnd 3: Ch 3, 2 dc in next sc, *dc in next sc, 2 dc in next sc, rep from * around, join in 3rd ch of beg ch-3. *(36 dc)*

Rnd 4: Ch 1, sc in same ch as beg ch-1, sc in next dc, 2 sc in next dc, *sc in each of next 2 dc, 2 sc in next dc, rep from * around, join in beg sc. *(48 sc)*

Rnd 5: Ch 3, dc in each of next 2 sc, 2 dc in next sc, *dc in each of next 3 sc, 2 dc in next sc, rep from * around, join in 3rd ch of beg ch-3. *(60 dc)*

Rnd 6: Ch 1, sc in same ch as beg ch-1, sc in each of next 3 dc, 2 sc in next dc, *sc in each of next 4 sc, 2 sc in next sc, rep from * around, join in beg sc. *(72 sc)*

Rnd 7: Ch 3, dc in each sc around, join in 3rd ch of beg ch-3.

Rnd 8: Ch 1, sc in each dc around, join in beg sc.

Rnds 9–16: [Rep rnds 7 and 8 alternately] 4 times.

Rnd 17: Rep rnd 7, **changing color** *(see Stitch Guide)* to toast in last dc.

Rnd 18: Ch 1, sc in same sc as beg ch-1, sc in next sc, ***fpdc** *(see Stitch Guide)* loosely around next dc on 2nd rnd below, sc in each of next 5 sc, rep from * 10 times, fpdc around next dc on 2nd rnd below, sc in each of next 3 sc, join in beg sc.

Rnd 19: Rep rnd 7, changing to black in last dc.

Rnd 20: Ch 1, sc in each of first 2 sc, fpdc around fpdc on 2nd rnd below, sc in each of next 5 sc, rep from * 10 times, fpdc around fpdc on 2nd rnd below, sc in each of last 3 sc, join in beg sc.

Rnd 21: Rep rnd 7, changing to toast in last dc.

Rnd 22: Rep rnd 20.

Rnd 23: Ch 2 *(see Pattern Notes)*, hdc in each st around, join in 2nd ch of beg ch-2. Fasten off.

Scarf

Note: *Scarf is worked from side to side.*

Row 1 (RS): With toast, ch 226, sc in 2nd ch from hook, sc in each rem ch across, turn. *(225 sc)*

Row 2: Ch 3 *(see Pattern Notes)*, dc in each sc across, **changing color** *(see Stitch Guide)* to black in last dc, turn.

Row 3: Ch 1, sc in first dc, ***fpdc** *(see Stitch Guide)* loosely around next sc on 2nd row below, sc in each of next 5 dc, rep from * to last 3 sts, fpdc around next sc on 2nd row below, sc in next dc, sc in 3rd ch of beg ch-3, turn.

Row 4: Rep row 2, changing color to toast in last dc.

Row 5: Ch 1, sc in first dc, *fpdc around next fpdc on 2nd row below, sc in each of next 5 sc, rep from * to last 3 sts, fpdc around next fpdc on 2nd row below, sc in next dc, sc in 3rd ch of beg ch-3, turn.

Row 6: Rep row 2.

Row 7: Rep row 5.

Row 8: Rep row 2, changing color to toast in last dc.

Rows 9–16: [Rep rows 5–8 consecutively] twice.

Row 17: Ch 3, dc in each sc across, turn.

Row 18: Ch 2 *(see Pattern Notes)*, hdc in each dc across, turn.

Row 19: Ch 1, sl st in each hdc across. Fasten off.

Side Edging

Hold piece with RS facing and 1 short end at top, **join** *(see Pattern Notes)* toast in end of first row in upper right-hand corner, work 22 sc evenly sp across side. Fasten off. Rep on 2nd short side. ●

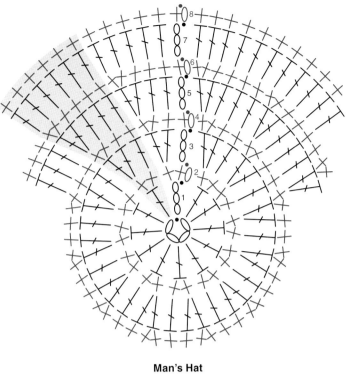

Man's Hat
Stitch Diagram Rnds 1–8
Note: Reps shown in gray.

STITCH KEY
⬭ Chain (ch)
• Slip stitch (sl st)
+ Single crochet (sc)
† Double crochet (dc)
Front post double crochet (fpdc)

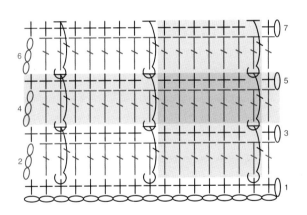

Man's Scarf
Reduced Sample of Stitch Diagram Rows 1–7
Note: Reps shown in gray.

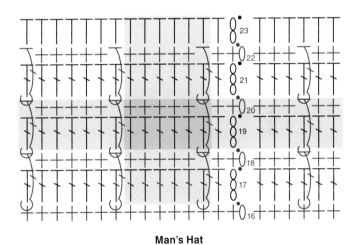

Man's Hat
Stitch Diagram Rnds 16–23
Note: Reps shown in gray.

City Girl Hat & Scarf

Designs by Jennifer Raymond

Skill Level

Hat:

 EXPERIENCED

Scarf:

 EASY

Finished Sizes

Hat: Instructions given fit child's size small; changes for child's sizes medium, large and adult's sizes small, medium and large are in [ ].

Scarf: One size fits most.

Finished Measurements

Hat circumference: 16 inches (*child's small*) [18 inches (*child's medium*), 20 inches (*child's large*), 22 inches (*adult's small*), 23 inches (*adult's medium*), 24 inches (*adult's large*)]

Hat length: 6½ inches (*child's small*) [7 inches (*child's medium*), 7½ inches (*child's large*), 8 inches (*adult's small*), 8½ inches (*adult's medium*), 9 inches (*adult's large*)]

Scarf: Approximately 6¾ inches wide x 75 inches long

Materials

- Plymouth Yarn Encore DK light (light worsted) weight acrylic/wool yarn (1¾ oz/150 yds/50g per ball): 7 [7, 7, 8, 8, 8] balls #0194 medium grey
- Size E/4/3.5mm crochet hook or size needed to obtain gauge
- Tapestry needle
- Stitch markers: 2, each a different color

Gauge

Hat: 24 sc = 4 inches; 28 rows = 4 inches

Scarf: 18 sts = 4 inches; 18 rows = 4 inches

Pattern Notes

Refer to Stitch Diagrams as needed.

Weave in loose ends as work progresses.

Work foundation chain loosely because it will affect the drape and stretch of the hat if the chain is too tight. If your chain is typically tighter than the rest of your crochet, make the chain with a hook 2 or 3 sizes larger than the hook used for the rest of the Hat.

Short rows are worked in order to create Wedges. In crochet, this creates a step and can create a hole between stitches. This hole is closed by working a single crochet decrease across the step. To maintain stitch count, a single crochet is also worked in the same stitch as the second leg of the single crochet decrease.

Extra-short rows are also used to create an even flare to the brim of the Hat as described in the Special Technique section. These short row flares are worked at the same time as the regular pattern rows. The flares are independent of the Wedge designation and are placed after every 12 rows (or 6 ridges). These extra-short rows are not counted in the overall row count.

Slip stitches are included in stitch counts.

Special Technique

Short row flare: Work short row flare after every 12 rows (*6 ridges*) as follows:

First flare row: Ch 1, sc in each of next 9 sts, sl st in next st, turn, leaving rem sts unworked.

Next flare row: Ch 1, sc in each sc across.

Hat

First Wedge

Row 1: Leaving long beg tail, **ch 49 [53, 57, 61, 63, 65] loosely** *(see Pattern Notes)*, working in **back bar of ch** *(see illustration)*, sc in 2nd ch from hook and in each rem ch across to last ch, sl st in last ch, turn. *(48 [52, 56, 60, 62, 64] sts)*

Back Bar of Chain

Row 2: Ch 1, working in **back lps** *(see Stitch Guide)*, sl st in first sc, sc in next st, place marker, sc in each rem st across, turn. *(47 [51, 55, 59, 61, 63] sts)*

Note: Work rem rows in back lps unless otherwise stated.

Row 3: Ch 1, sc in each st across to marker, sl st in marked st, turn. *(46 [50, 54, 58, 60, 62] sts)*

Rows 4–7: [Rep rows 2 and 3 alternately] twice. *(42 [46, 50, 54, 56, 58] sts at end of last row)*

Row 8: Ch 1, sl st in first sc, sc in each of next 2 sts, place marker, sc in each rem st across, turn. *(41 [45, 49, 53, 55, 57] sts at end of last row)*

Row 9: Rep row 3. *(39 [43, 47, 51, 53, 55] sts)*

Row 10: Rep row 8. *(38 [42, 46, 50, 52, 54] sts)*

Row 11: Rep row 3. *(36 [40, 44, 48, 50, 52] sts)*

Row 12: Rep row 8. *(35 [39, 43, 47, 49, 51] sts)*

*Note: Work **short row flare** (see Special Technique and Pattern Notes). Continue to work short row flares after every 12 rows at the same time as working the regular pattern.*

Row 13: Ch 1, sc in each st across to next sl st, **sc dec** *(see Stitch Guide and Pattern Notes)* in sl st and next unworked st on row 12, sc in same st as last leg of sc dec worked, sc in each rem unworked st on row 12

to marker, sl st in marked st, turn. *(33 [37, 41, 45, 47, 49] sts)*

Row 14: Rep row 8. *(32 [36, 40, 44, 46, 48] sts)*

Row 15: Rep row 3. *(30 [34, 38, 42, 44, 46] sts)*

Row 16: Rep row 8. *(29 [33, 37, 41, 43, 45] sts)*

Row 17: Rep row 3. *(27 [31, 35, 39, 41, 43] sts)*

Row 18: Rep row 8. *(26 [30, 34, 38, 40, 42] sts)*

Row 19: Rep row 3. *(24 [28, 32, 36, 38, 40] sts)*

Rows 20 & 21: Rep rows 2 and 3. *(22 [26, 30, 34, 36, 38] sts)*

Row 22: Rep row 8. *(21 [25, 29, 33, 35, 37] sts)*

Sizes Child's Small & Medium Only

2nd Wedge

Row 1: Ch 1, sc in each st across to next sl st, working across ends of rows, sc dec in sl st and sl st on next row, sc in same st as last leg of sc dec worked, [sc dec in next 2 sl sts, sc in same st as last leg of sc dec worked, sc in next unworked sc] 6 times, [sc dec in next 2 sl sts, sc in same st as last leg of sc dec worked] 3 times, sc dec in last 2 sl sts, sl st in same st as last leg of sc dec worked, turn. *(48 [52] sts)*

Rep rem rows of First Wedge, working a short row flare after every 12th Wedge row from last short row flare.

3rd–5th Wedges

Work same as 2nd Wedge.

Next row: Rep row 1 of 2nd Wedge.

Last row: Ch 1, sl st in first sc, sc in each rem st across. Fasten off.

Continue with Finishing.

Size Child's Large Only

Row [23]: Rep row 3. *([28] sts)*

Row [24]: Rep row 2. *([27] sts)*

2nd Wedge
Row [1]: Ch 1, sc in each st across to next sl st, working across next ends of rows, sc dec in sl st and sl st on next row, sc in same st as last leg of sc dec worked, sc dec in next 2 sl sts, sc in same st as last leg of sc dec worked, sc in next unworked sc, [sc dec in next 2 sl sts, sc in same st as last leg of sc dec worked, sc in next unworked sc] 6 times, [sc dec in next 2 sl sts, sc in same st as last leg of sc dec worked] 3 times, sc dec in last 2 sl sts, sl st in same st as last leg of sc dec worked, turn. *([56] sts)*

Rep rem rows of First Wedge, working a short row flare after every 12th Wedge row from last short row flare.

3rd–5th Wedges
Work same as 2nd Wedge.

Next row: Rep row 1 of 2nd Wedge.

Last row: Ch 1, sl st in first sc, sc in each rem st across. Fasten off.

Continue with Finishing.

Sizes Adult's Small & Medium Only
Row [23]: Rep row 3. *([32, 34] sts)*

Row [24]: Rep row 2. *([31, 33] sts)*

Row [25]: Rep row 3. *([30, 32] sts)*

Row [26]: Rep row 8. *([29, 31] sts)*

2nd Wedge
Row [1]: Ch 1, sc in each st across to next sl st, working across ends of rows, sc dec in sl st and sl st on next row, sc in same st as last leg of sc dec worked, [sc dec in next 2 sl sts, sc in same st as last leg of sc dec worked] twice, sc dec in next 2 sl sts, sc in same st as last leg of sc dec worked, sc in next unworked sc] 6 times, [sc dec in next 2 sl sts, sc in same st as last leg of sc dec worked] 3 times, sc dec

in last 2 sl sts, sl st in same st as last leg of sc dec worked, turn. *([60, 62] sts)*

Rep rem rows of First Wedge, working a short row flare after every 12th Wedge row from last short row flare.

3rd–5th Wedges
Work same as 2nd Wedge.

Next row: Rep row 1 of 2nd Wedge.

Last row: Ch 1, sl st in first sc, sc in each rem st across. Fasten off.

Continue with Finishing.

Size Adult's Large Only
Row [23]: Rep row 3. *([36] sts)*

Row [24]: Rep row 2. *([35] sts)*

Row [25]: Rep row 3. *([34] sts)*

Row [26]: Rep row 8. *([33] sts)*

Row [27]: Rep row 3. *([31] sts)*

Row [28]: Rep row 8. *([30] sts)*

2nd Wedge
Row [1]: Ch 1, sc in each st across to next sl st, working across ends of rows, sc dec in sl st and sl st on next row, sc in same st as last leg of sc dec worked, sc in next unworked sc, [sc dec in next 2 sl sts, sc in same st as last leg of sc dec worked] 3 times, [sc dec in next 2 sl sts, sc in same st as last leg of sc dec worked, sc in next unworked sc] 6 times, [sc dec in next 2 sl sts, sc in same st as last leg of sc dec worked] 3 times, sc dec in last 2 sl sts, sl st in same st as last leg of sc dec worked, turn. *([64] sts)*

Rep rem rows of First Wedge, working a short row flare after every 12th Wedge row from last short row flare.

3rd–5th Wedges

Work same as 2nd Wedge.

Next row: Rep row 1 of 2nd Wedge.

Last row: Ch 1, sl st in first sc, sc in each rem st across. Fasten off.

Finishing

Weave beg tail through each st at crown, pull tight to close. Sew first row and last row tog.

Scarf

Row 1 (RS): Ch 271 sts, sc in **back bar** (*see illustration*) of 2nd ch from hook and in each rem ch across, turn. (*270 sc*)

Back Bar of Chain

Row 2: Ch 1, working in **back lps** (*see Stitch Guide*), sc in each sc across, turn.

Row 3: Ch 1, working in back lps, sc in each of first 10 sc, [ch 5, sk next 5 sc, sc in each of next 5 sc] 25 times, leaving rem sts unworked, turn.

Note: *On rem rows, work sc through both lps of chs and work sc in back lps of sc.*

Row 4: Ch 11, sk first ch from hook, sc in each of next 10 chs, sc in each st across, turn. (*270 sc*)

Row 5: Ch 1, sc in each sc across, turn.

Row 6: Ch 1, sc in each of first 10 sc, [ch 5, sk next 5 sc, sc in each of next 5 sc] 25 times, leaving rem sts unworked, turn.

Rows 7–45: [Rep rows 4–6 consecutively] 13 times.

Rows 46 & 47: Rep rows 4 and 5. At end of last row, fasten off.

Finishing

Block to desired dimensions. ●

STITCH KEY	
◯	Chain (ch)
•	Slip stitch (sl st)
+	Single crochet (sc)
⋏	Single crochet decrease (sc dec)
⌢	Worked in back lp

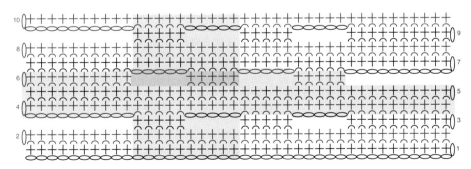

City Girl Scarf
Reduced Sample of Stitch Diagram
Note: *Reps shown in gray.*

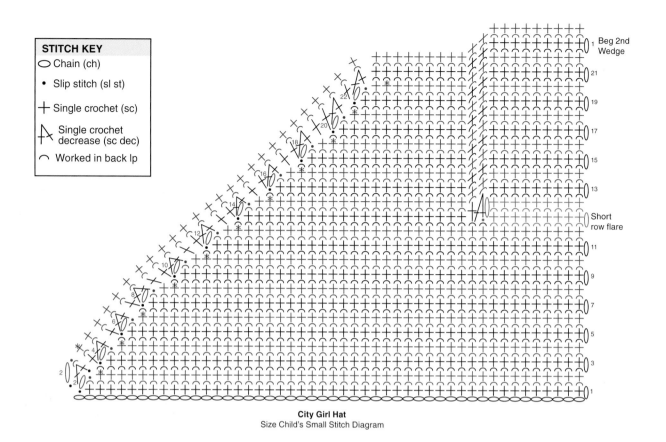

City Girl Hat
Size Child's Small Stitch Diagram

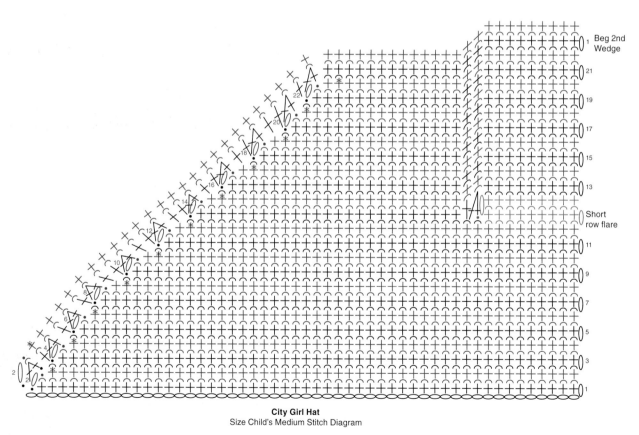

City Girl Hat
Size Child's Medium Stitch Diagram

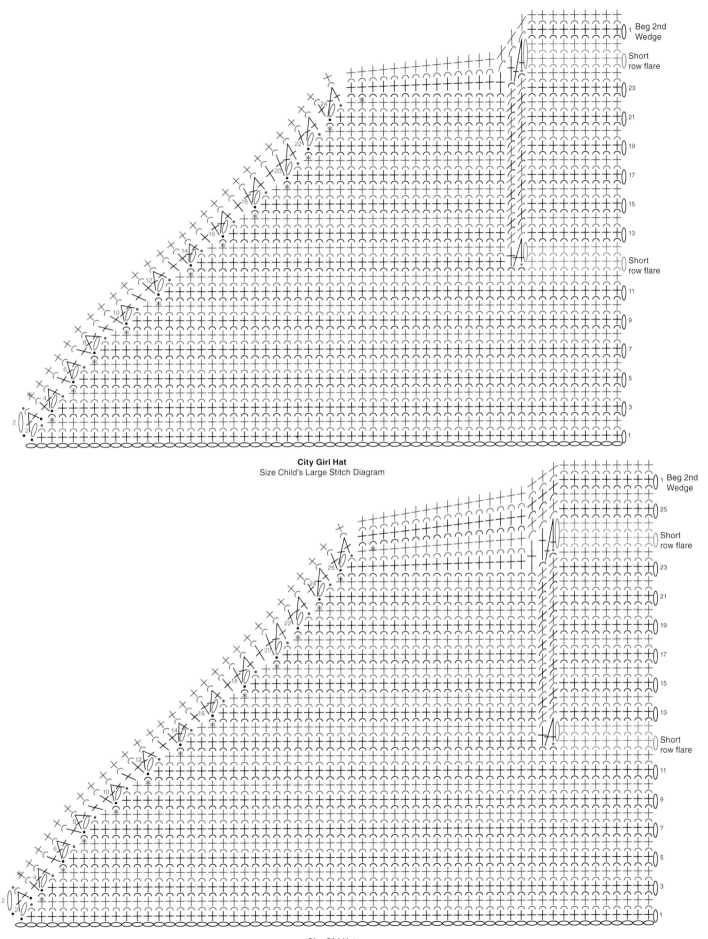

City Girl Hat
Size Child's Large Stitch Diagram

City Girl Hat
Size Adult's Small Stitch Diagram

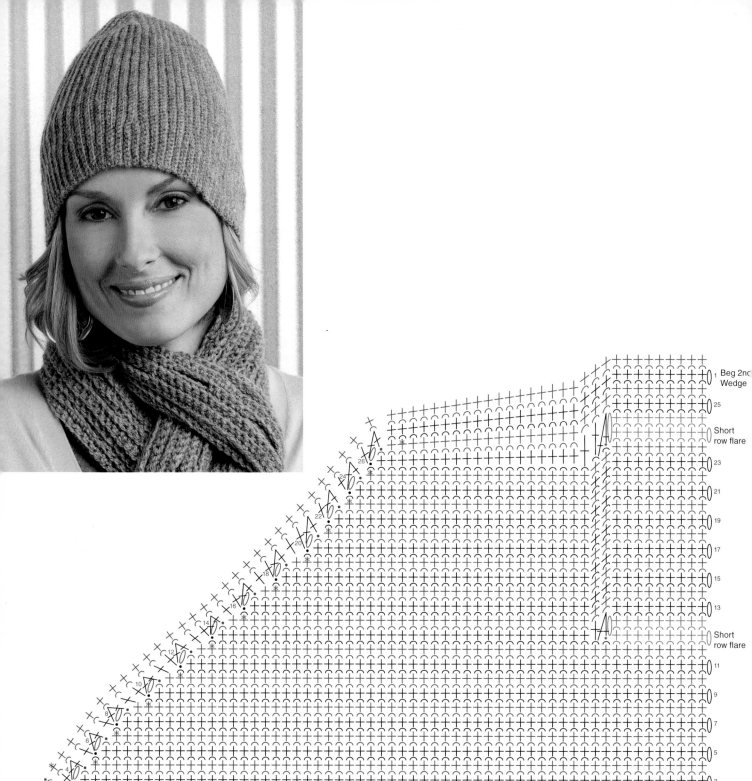

City Girl Hat
Size Adult's Medium Stitch Diagram

STITCH KEY

○ Chain (ch)

• Slip stitch (sl st)

+ Single crochet (sc)

⩗ Single crochet decrease (sc dec)

⌒ Worked in back lp

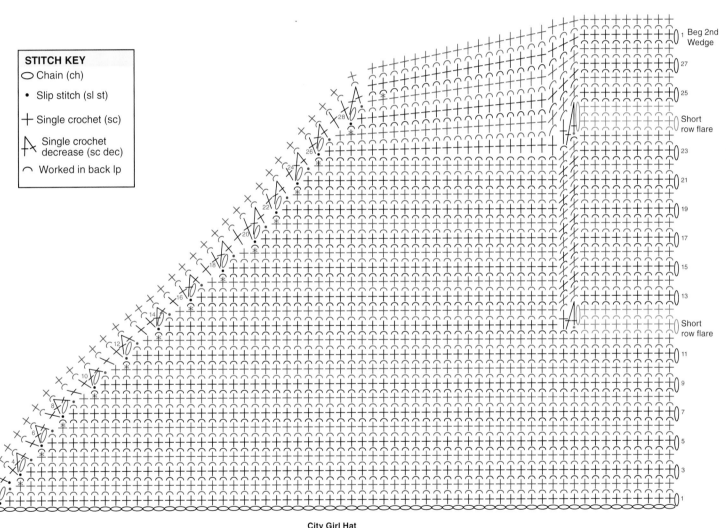

City Girl Hat
Size Adult's Large Stitch Diagram

Man's Camo Hat & Scarf

Designs by Glenda Winkleman

Skill Level

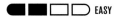 **■■□□** EASY

Finished Measurements

Hat: 21 inches in circumference

Scarf: 5¼ inches x 66 inches

Materials

- Red Heart Classic medium (worsted) weight acrylic yarn (3 oz/146 yds/85g per skein): 5 skeins #971 camouflage
- Size I/9/5.5mm crochet hook or size needed to obtain gauge
- Tapestry needle
- Stitch marker

Gauge

Hat: Rnds 1 and 2 = 1½ inches

Scarf: 13 sc = 4 inches; 18 sc rows = 4 inches

Pattern Notes

Refer to Stitch Diagrams as needed.

Weave in loose ends as work progresses.

Hat is worked in continuous rounds. Do not join unless specified. Place marker at beginning of round; move marker up as work progresses.

Scarf is worked lengthwise.

Hat

Rnd 1 (RS): Beg at top, ch 2, 6 sc in 2nd ch from hook. (6 sc)

Rnd 2: Place marker (see Pattern Notes), (sc, dc) in each sc around. (12 sts)

Rnd 3: *(Sc, dc) in next sc, sc in next dc, rep from * around. (18 sts)

Rnd 4: (Sc, dc) in next sc, sc in next dc, *dc in next sc, (sc, dc) in next sc, sc in next dc, rep from * around to last sc, dc in last sc. (24 sts)

Rnd 5: Rep rnd 3. (36 sts)

Rnd 6: Rep rnd 4. (48 sts)

Rnd 7: *(Sc, dc) in next sc, sc in next dc, dc in next sc, sc in next dc, rep from * around. (60 sts)

Rnd 8: *Dc in next st, sc in next st, rep from * around.

Rnd 9: *Sc in next dc, dc in next sc, rep from * around.

Rnd 10: *Dc in next sc, sc in next dc, rep from * around.

Rnds 11–24: [Rep rnds 9 and 10 alternately] 7 times. At end of last rnd, join with sl st in first dc. Fasten off.

Brim

Row 1: Ch 10, sc in 2nd ch from hook, sc in each rem ch across, turn. (9 sc)

Row 2: Ch 1, sc in **back lp** (see Stitch Guide) of each sc across, turn.

Rows 3–60: Rep row 2. At end of last row, fasten off.

Assembly

With tapestry needle, sew last row of Brim to edge of foundation ch. Having seam at center back, sew 1 long edge of Brim to last rnd of Hat.

Scarf

Row 1 (RS): Ch 215, sc in 2nd ch from hook, sc in each rem ch across, turn. *(214 sc)*

Row 2: Ch 1, working in **back lps** *(see Stitch Guide)* only, sc in each sc across, turn.

Rows 3–20: Rep row 2.

Border

Working through both lps, sc in each sc across to next corner, ch 2, working across next side in ends of rows, work 12 sc evenly sp across to next corner, ch 2, working across next side in unused lps of starting ch, sc in each lp across, ch 2, working across next side in ends of rows, work 12 sc evenly sp across to next corner, ch 2, join with sl st in beg sc. Fasten off. ●

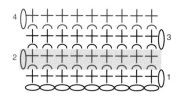

Man's Camo Scarf
Reduced Sample of Stitch Diagram Rows 1–4
Note: Rep shown in gray.

STITCH KEY	
◯	Chain (ch)
+	Single crochet (sc)
⊤	Double crochet (dc)
⌒	Worked in back lp

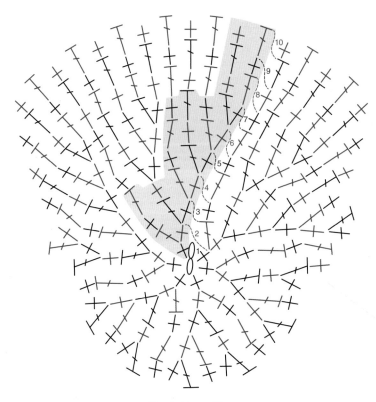

Man's Camo Hat
Stitch Diagram Rnds 1–10
Note: Reps shown in gray.

Snowball Hat & Scarf

Designs by Kathleen Stuart

Skill Level

 EASY

Finished Measurements

Hat: 20 inches in circumference

Scarf: 6 inches wide x 49 inches long

Materials

- Plymouth Yarn Encore Tweed medium (worsted) weight acrylic/wool/rayon yarn (3½ oz/200 yds/100g per ball):
    - 2 balls #T520 dark grey
    - 1 ball #T789 grey
- Size J/10/6mm crochet hook or size needed to obtain gauge
- Tapestry needle
- Stitch markers

Gauge

11 sts = 4 inches

Pattern Notes

Refer to Stitch Diagrams as needed.

Weave in loose ends as work progresses.

Hat is worked in continuous rounds. Do not join unless specified. Place marker at beginning of round; move marker up as work progresses.

Scarf is worked lengthwise.

Chain-2 at beginning of round counts as a double crochet unless otherwise stated.

Join with slip stitch as indicated unless otherwise stated.

Chain-3 at beginning of row counts as a double crochet unless otherwise stated.

Special Stitches

Shell: 7 dc in indicated st.

Cluster (cl): Holding back last lp of each dc on hook, dc in each of 4 sts indicated, yo and draw through all 5 lps on hook.

7-double crochet cluster (7-dc cl): Holding back last lp of each dc on hook, dc in each of 7 sts indicated, yo and draw through all 8 lps on hook.

3-double crochet cluster (3-dc cl): Holding back last lp of each dc on hook, dc in each of 3 sts indicated, yo and draw through all 4 lps on hook.

Hat

Rnd 1: Beg at top with dark grey, ch 2, 6 sc in 2nd ch from hook. *(6 sc)*

Rnd 2: Place marker *(see Pattern Notes)*, (sc, dc) in each st around. *(12 sts)*

Rnd 3: [Dc in next st, (sc, dc) in next st] 6 times. *(18 sts)*

Rnd 4: *Sc in next st, dc in next st, (sc, dc) in next st, rep from * around. *(24 sts)*

Rnd 5: *Dc in next st, sc in next st, dc in next st, (sc, dc) in next st, rep from * around. *(30 sts)*

Rnd 6: *[Sc in next st, dc in next st] twice, (sc, dc) in next st, rep from * around. *(36 sts)*

Rnd 7: *[Dc in next st, sc in next st] twice, dc in next st, (sc, dc) in next st, rep from * around. *(42 sts)*

Rnd 8: *[Sc in next st, dc in next st] 3 times, (sc, dc) in next st, rep from * around. *(48 sts)*

Rnd 9: *[Dc in next st, sc in next st] 3 times, dc in next st, (sc, dc) in next st, rep from * around. *(54 sts)*

Rnd 10: *[Sc in next st, dc in next st] 4 times, (sc, dc) in next st, rep from * around. *(60 sts)*

Rnd 11: *Dc in next st, sc in next st, rep from * around.

Rnd 12: *Sc in next st, dc in next st, rep from * around.

Rnds 13–16: [Rep rnds 11 and 12] twice.

Rnd 17: Sc in first 2 sts; *sk next 3 sts, **shell** *(see Special Stitches)* in next st, sk next 3 sts, sc in each of next 3 sts, rep from * 4 times, sk next 3 sts, shell in next st, sk next 3 sts, sc in last st, change color to grey by drawing lp through, cut dark grey. *(6 shells)*

Rnd 18: Sl st in first sc, **ch 2** *(see Pattern Notes)*, **cl** *(see Special Stitches)* in same st as beg ch-2 and in next 3 sts, *ch 3, sc in each of next 3 sts, ch 3, **7-dc cl** *(see Special Stitches)* in next 7 sts, rep from * around to last 6 sts, ch 3, sc in each of next 3 sts, ch 3, **3-dc cl** *(see Special Stitches)* in last 3 sts, **join** *(see Pattern Notes)* in 2nd ch of beg ch-2.

Rnd 19: Ch 2, 3 dc in next st, *sk next ch-3 sp, sc in each of next 3 sts, sk next ch-3 sp, shell in next st, rep from * around to last 2 ch-3 sps, sk next ch-3 sp, sc in each of next 3 sts, sk last ch-3 sp, 3 dc in next st, change color to dark grey by drawing lp through, cut grey, join with sc in 2nd ch of beg ch-2.

Rnd 20: Sc in next st, *ch 3, 7-dc cl in next 7 sts, ch 3, sc in each of next 3 sts, rep from * around to last 8 sts, ch 3, 7-dc cl in next 7 sts, ch 3, sc in last st.

Rnd 21: Working in **back lps** *(see Stitch Guide)*, *sc in each of next 9 sts, 2 sc in next st, rep from * around. *(66 sc)*

Rnd 22: *[Sc in next st, dc in next st] 5 times, (sc, dc) in next st, rep from * around. *(72 sts)*

Rnd 23: *[Dc in next st, sc in next st] 5 times, dc in next st, (sc, dc) in next st, rep from * around. *(78 sts)*

Rnd 24: *[Sc in next st, dc in next st] 6 times, (sc, dc) in next st, rep from * around. *(84 sts)*

Rnd 25: *Dc in next st, sc in next st, rep from * around.

Rnd 26: *Sc in next st, dc in next st, rep from * around.

Rnd 27: Ch 1, working from left to right, work **reverse sc** (see Stitch Guide) in each st, join in beg reverse sc. Fasten off

Scarf

Row 1: With dark grey, ch 152, sc in 2nd ch from hook, *dc in next ch, sc in next ch, rep from * across, turn. *(151 sts)*

Row 2: Ch 3 (see Pattern Notes), *sc in next st, dc in next st, rep from * across, turn.

Row 3: Ch 1, sc in first st, *dc in next st, sc in next st, rep from * across, turn.

Rows 4 & 5: Rep rows 2 and 3.

Row 6: Ch 1, sc in each of first 2 sts, *sk next 3 sts, **shell** (see Special Stitches) in next st, sk next 3 sts, sc in each of next 3 sts, rep from * across to last 9 sts, sk next 3 sts, shell in next st, sk next 3 sts, sc in each of last 2 sts, change color to grey by drawing lp through, cut dark grey, turn.

Row 7: Ch 2, **cl** (see Special Stitches) in first 4 sts, *ch 3, sc in each of next 3 sts, ch 3, **7-dc cl** (see Special Stitches) in next 7 sts, rep from * across to last 7 sts, ch 3, sc in each of next 3 sts, ch 3, cl in last 4 sts, turn.

Row 8: Ch 2, 4 dc in first st, *sk next ch-3 sp, sc in next 3 sts, sk next ch-3 sp, shell in next st, rep from * across to last 2 ch-3 sps, sk next ch-3 sp, sc in each of next 3 sts, sk last ch-3 sp, 4 dc in next st, change color to dark grey by drawing lp through, cut grey, turn, leaving beg ch-2 unworked.

Row 9: Ch 1, sc in each of first 2 sts, *ch 3, 7-dc cl in next 7 sts, ch 3, sc in each of next 3 sts, rep from * across to last 9 sts, ch 3, 7-dc cl in next 7 sts, ch 3, sc in each of last 2 sts, turn.

Row 10: Ch 1, sc in first st, *dc in next st, sc in next ch, dc in next ch, sc in next ch, dc in next ch, sc in next ch, dc in next ch, sc in next ch, dc in next st, sc in next st, rep from * across, turn.

Rows 11–14: [Rep rows 2 and 3] twice. At end of last row, fasten off. ●

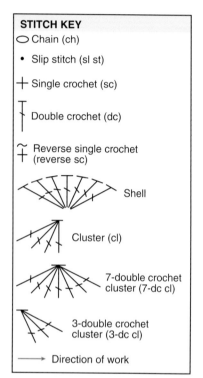

STITCH KEY
- ◯ Chain (ch)
- • Slip stitch (sl st)
- ┼ Single crochet (sc)
- ╤ Double crochet (dc)
- ╤̃ Reverse single crochet (reverse sc)
- Shell
- Cluster (cl)
- 7-double crochet cluster (7-dc cl)
- 3-double crochet cluster (3-dc cl)
- ⟶ Direction of work

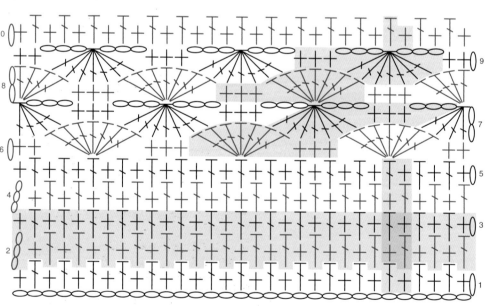

Snowball Scarf
Reduced Sample of Stitch Diagram Rnds 1–11
Note: Reps shown in gray.

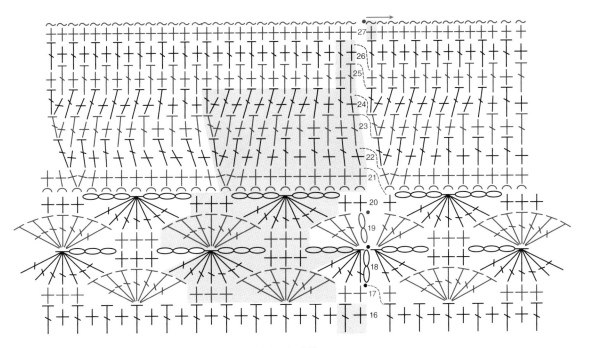

Snowball Hat
Reduced Sample of Stitch Diagram Rnds 16–27
Note: *Reps shown in gray.*

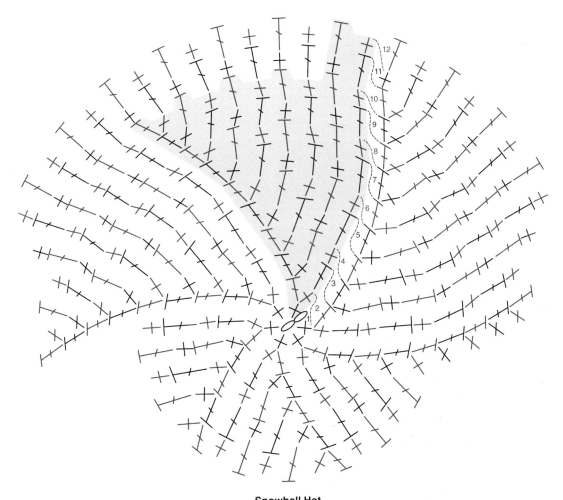

Snowball Hat
Reduced Sample of Stitch Diagram Rnds 1–12
Note: *Reps shown in gray.*

Fun & Funky Half-Hats

Designs by Jennifer Cirka

Skill Level

 INTERMEDIATE

Finished Measurements

Adult: 21 inches in circumference

Child: 19 inches in circumference

Materials

Adult

- Patons Kroy Socks FX super fine (sock) weight wool/nylon yarn (1¾ oz/166 yds/50g per ball): 1 ball #57242 clover colors

- Patons Shetland Chunky bulky (chunky) weight acrylic/wool yarn (3½ oz/148 yds/100g per ball): 1 ball #78108 medium blue

Child

- Patons Kroy Socks super fine (sock) weight wool/nylon yarn (1¾ oz/166 yds/50g per ball): 1 ball #55616 mulberry stripes
- Patons Beehive Baby Chunky bulky (chunky) weight acrylic/nylon (3½ oz/120 yds/100g per ball): 1 ball #76421 plusher pink

Both Sizes

- Size K/10½/6.5mm crochet hook or size needed to obtain gauge
- Tapestry needle
- Pompom maker

Gauge

With chunky yarn: 10 sc = 4 inches; 13 sc rows = 4 inches

Pattern Notes

Refer to Stitch Diagrams as needed.

Weave in ends as work progresses.

Join with slip stitch as indicated unless otherwise stated.

Special Stitches

First foundation single crochet (first foundation sc): Ch 2, insert hook into 2nd ch from hook, yo, pull up lp, yo, pull through 1 lp on hook *(see illustration A—ch-1 completed)*, yo, pull through all lps on hook *(see illustrations B and C—sc completed)*.

A

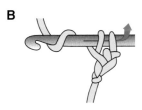

B

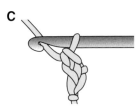

C

**First Foundation
Single Crochet**

Next foundation single crochet (next foundation sc): [Insert hook in last ch-1 made, yo, pull up lp, yo, pull through 1 lp on hook *(see illustrations A and B— ch-1 completed)*, yo, pull through all lps on hook *(see illustrations C and D—sc completed)*] as many times as indicated in instructions.

A

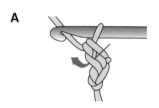

B

C

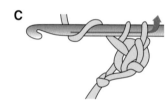

D

**Next Foundation
Single Crochet**

Cluster (cl): Holding back last lp of each st on hook, 5 dc in indicated st or sp, yo, pull through all lps on hook. Push cl to RS of work.

Adult Hat

Rnd 1: With blue, work **first foundation sc** *(see Special Stitches)*, work 47 **next foundation sc** *(see Special Stitches)*, **join** *(see Pattern Notes)* in first st. *(48 sts)*

Rnd 2 (RS): Ch 1, sc in each of first 7 sts, 2 sc in next st, [sc in each of next 7 sts, 2 sc in next st] around, **changing colors** *(see Stitch Guide)* to clover colors in last st, join in beg sc, **turn**. *(54 sc)*

Rnd 3 (WS): Ch 2, **cl** *(see Special Stitches)* in first st, sk next st, dc in next st, working around last dc worked, dc in sk st, [cl in next st, sk next st, dc in next st, working around last dc worked, dc in sk st] around, changing color to blue in last st, join in beg cl, turn. *(18 cls, 36 dc)*

Rnd 4: Ch 1, sc in each st around, join in beg sc, **do not turn**.

Rnd 5: Ch 1, sc in each st around, join in beg sc.

Rnd 6: Ch 1, sc in each st around, changing color to clover colors in last st, join in beg sc, turn.

Rnds 7–9: Rep rnds 3–5. At end of last rnd, fasten off.

First Earflap

Row 1: Sk first 5 sts on last rnd, join blue with sc in next st, sc in each of next 11 sts, leaving rem sts unworked, turn. *(12 sc)*

Row 2: Ch 1, sc in each st across, turn.

Row 3: Ch 1, **sc dec** *(see Stitch Guide)* in first 2 sts, sc in each st across to last 2 sts, sc dec in last 2 sts, turn. *(10 sc)*

Rows 4 & 5: Rep rows 2 and 3. *(8 sc)*

Row 6: Rep row 2.

Rows 7 & 8: Rep row 3. *(4 sc)*

Row 9: Ch 1, sc in first st, ch 1, sk next 2 sts, sc in last st. Fasten off. *(2 sc)*

2nd Earflap

Row 1: Sk next 20 sts on last rnd from First Earflap, join blue with sc in next st, sc in each of next 11 sts, leaving rem sts unworked, turn. *(12 sc)*

Rows 2–9: Rep rows 2–9 of First Earflap.

Pompom

Using pompom maker and clover colors, make 2 large Pompoms.

Finishing

Cut 18 strands of blue each 32 inches long. Using 9 strands per side, fold and attach yarn through ch-1 sp at end of each Earflap. Dividing strands into 3 groups, braid strands. Secure and trim ends.

Attach 1 Pompom to bottom of each braid.

Child Hat

Rnd 1: With pink, work **first foundation sc** *(see Special Stitches)*, work 41 **next foundation sc** *(see Special Stitches)*, **join** *(see Pattern Note)* in first sc. *(42 sc)*

Rnd 2 (RS): Ch 1, sc in each of first 6 sts, 2 sc in next st, [sc in each of next 6 sts, 2 sc in next st] around, **changing colors** *(see Stitch Guide)* to mulberry stripes in last st, join in beg sc, **turn**. *(48 sc)*

Rnd 3 (WS): Ch 2, **cl** *(see Special Stitches)* in first st, sk next st, dc in next st, working around last dc worked, dc in sk st, [cl in next st, sk next st, dc in next st, working around last dc worked, dc in sk st] around, changing to pink in last st, join in beg cl, turn. *(16 cls, 32 dc)*

Rnd 4: Ch 1, sc in each st around, join in beg sc, **do not turn**.

Rnd 5: Ch 1, sc in each st around, changing to mulberry stripes in last st, join in beg sc, turn.

Rnds 6 & 7: Rep rnds 3 and 4.

Rnd 8: Ch 1, sc in each st around, join in beg sc. Fasten off.

First Earflap

Row 1: Sk first 5 sts on last rnd, join pink with sc in next st, sc in each of next 9 sts, leaving rem sts unworked, turn. *(10 sc)*

Row 2: Ch 1, sc in each st across, turn.

Row 3: Ch 1, **sc dec** *(see Stitch Guide)* in first 2 sts, sc in each st across to last 2 sts, sc dec in last 2 sts, turn. *(8 sc)*

Rows 4 & 5: Rep rows 2 and 3. *(6 sc)*

Row 6: Rep row 2.

Row 7: Rep row 3. *(4 sc)*

Row 8: Ch 1, sc in first st, sk next 2 sts, sc in last st. Fasten off.

2nd Earflap

Row 1: Sk next 18 sts from First Earflap on last rnd of Hat, join pink with sc in next st, sc in each of next 9 sts, leaving rem sts unworked, turn. *(10 sc)*

Rows 2–8: Rep rows 2–8 of First Earflap.

Pompom

Using pompom maker and mulberry stripes, make 2 large Pompoms.

Finishing

Cut 18 strands of pink each 32 inches long. Using 9 strands per side, fold and attach yarn through ch-1 sp at end of each Earflap. Dividing strands into 3 groups, braid strands. Secure and trim ends.

Attach 1 Pompom to bottom of each braid. ●

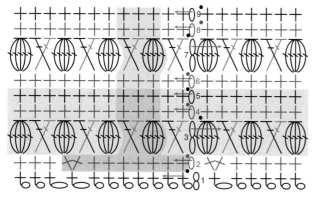

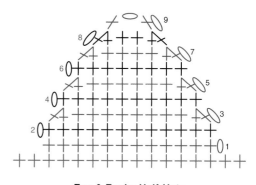

Fun & Funky Half-Hats
Adult Hat Stitch Diagram
Note: Reps shown in gray.

Fun & Funky Half-Hats
Adult Hat Earflap Stitch Diagram

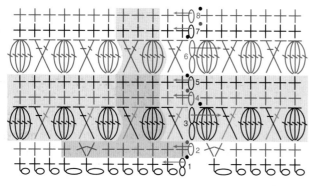

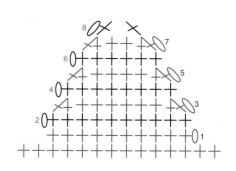

Fun & Funky Half-Hats
Child Hat Stitch Diagram
Note: Reps shown in gray.

Fun & Funky Half-Hats
Child Hat Earflap Stitch Diagram

STITCH KEY

◯ Chain (ch)

• Slip stitch (sl st)

+ Single crochet (sc)

┬ Double crochet (dc)

First foundation single crochet (first foundation sc)

Next foundation single crochet (next foundation sc)

Cluster (cl)

⇄ Direction of work

Snow Crest

Designs by Lisa Naskrent

Skill Level

 INTERMEDIATE

Finished Sizes

Instructions given fit toddler (2–4 years); changes for child (5–7 years), tween (8–12 years), woman and man are in [ ].

Finished Measurements

Hat: 17 inches (toddler) [19 inches (child), 19 inches (tween), 20½ inches (woman), 22½ inches (man)] in circumference

Scarf: 3 inches wide x 36 inches long (toddler) [5 inches wide x 42 inches long (child), 5 inches wide x 48 inches long (tween), 7 inches wide x 60 inches long (woman), 9 x 72 inches (man)]

Mittens: Palm to fingertip: 4½ inches (toddler) [5½ inches (child), 6¼ inches (tween), 7¼ inches (woman), 8¼ inches (man)]

Materials

- Lion Brand Wool-Ease medium (worsted) weight acrylic/wool yarn (3 oz/197 yds/85g per skein): 3 [3, 3, 4, 6] balls #139 dark rose heather
- Size I/9/5.5mm crochet hook or size needed to obtain gauge
- Tapestry needle
- Stitch marker

Gauge

Hat: 2 shells and 2 ch-2 sps = 3¾ inches; 7 pattern rows = 3¾ inches

Pattern Notes

Refer to Stitch Diagrams as needed.

Weave in loose ends as work progresses.

Join with slip stitch as indicated unless otherwise stated.

Chain-3 at beginning of round counts as a double crochet unless otherwise stated.

Special Stitches

Beginning half shell (beg half shell): Ch 3 *(see Pattern Notes)*, 2 dc in indicated sp.

Half shell: 3 dc in indicated sp.

Shell: 5 dc in indicated sp.

Beginning shell (beg shell): Ch 3, 4 dc in indicated sp.

Hat

Rnd 1 (RS): Beg at top, ch 3, **join** *(see Pattern Notes)* in first ch to form ring, ch 1, [sc in ring, ch 2] 8 [10, 10, 10, 12] times, join in beg sc. *(8 [10, 10, 10, 12] sc, 8 [10, 10, 10, 12] ch-2 sps)*

Rnd 2: Sl st in next ch-2 sp, **beg half shell** *(see Special Stitches)* in same sp, (sc, ch 2, sc) in next ch-2 sp, ***half shell** (see Special Stitches) in next ch-2 sp, (sc, ch 2, sc) in next ch-2 sp, rep from * around, join in 3rd ch of beg ch-3. (4 [5, 5, 5, 6] half shells, 4 [5, 5, 5, 6] ch-2 sps)*

Rnd 3: Ch 1, [sc, ch 2] 3 times in next dc, sc in same dc, half shell in next ch-2 sp, *[sc, ch 2] 3 times in 2nd dc of next half shell, sc in same dc, half shell in next ch-2 sp, rep from * around, join in beg sc. *(4 [5, 5, 5, 6] half shells, 12 [15, 15, 15, 18] ch-2 sps)*

Sizes Toddler & Woman Only

Rnd 4: Sl st in first ch-2 sp, beg half shell in same sp, (sc, ch 2, sc) in next ch-2 sp, half shell in next ch-2 sp, [sc, ch 2] 3 times in 2nd dc of next half shell, sc in same dc, *half shell in next ch-2 sp, (sc, ch 2, sc) in next ch-2 sp, half shell in next ch-2 sp, (sc, ch 2, sc) in 2nd dc of next half shell, rep from * around, join in 3rd ch of beg ch-3. *(8 [10] half shells, 10 [12] ch-2 sps)*

Rnd 5: Ch 1, (sc, ch 2, sc) in next dc, half shell in next ch-2 sp, (sc, ch 2, sc) in 2nd dc of next half shell, half shell in next ch-2 sp, (sc, ch 2, sc) in next ch-2 sp, half shell in next ch-2 sp, *(sc, ch 2, sc) in 2nd dc of next half shell, half shell in next ch-2 sp, rep from * around, join in beg sc. *(9 [11] half shells, 9 [11] ch-2 sps)*

Continue with All Sizes.

Sizes Child, Tween & Man Only

Rnd [4]: Sl st in first ch-2 sp, beg half shell in same sp, (sc, ch 2, sc) in next ch-2 sp, half shell in next ch-2 sp, (sc, ch 2, sc) in 2nd dc of next half shell, *half shell in next ch-2 sp, (sc, ch 2, sc) in next ch-2 sp, half shell in next ch-2 sp, (sc, ch 2, sc) in 2nd dc of next half shell, rep from * around, join in 3rd ch of beg ch-3. *([10, 10, 12] half shells, [10, 10, 12] ch-2 sps)*

Rnd [5]: Ch 1, (sc, ch 2, sc) in next dc, half shell in next ch-2 sp, *(sc, ch 2, sc) in 2nd dc of next half shell, half shell in next ch-2 sp, rep from * around, join in beg sc. *([10, 10, 12] half shells, [10, 10, 12] ch-2 sps)*

Continue with All Sizes.

All Sizes

Rnd 6: Sl st in first ch-2 sp, beg half shell in same sp, (sc, ch 2, sc) in 2nd dc of next half shell, *half shell in next ch-2 sp, (sc, ch 2, sc) in 2nd dc of next half shell, rep from * around, join in 3rd ch of beg ch-3. *(9 [10, 10, 11, 12] half shells, 9 [10, 10, 11, 12] ch-2 sps)*

Rnd 7: Ch 1, (sc, ch 2, sc) in next dc, **shell** *(see Special Stitches)* in next ch-2 sp, *(sc, ch 2, sc) in 2nd dc of next half shell, shell in next ch-2 sp, rep from * around, join in beg sc. *(9 [10, 10, 11, 12] shells, 9 [10, 10, 11, 12] ch-2 sps)*

Rnd 8: Sl st in first ch-2 sp, **beg shell** *(see Special Stitches)* in same sp, (sc, ch 2, sc) in 3rd dc of next shell, *shell in next ch-2 sp, (sc, ch 2, sc) in 3rd dc of next shell, rep from * around, join in 3rd ch of beg ch-3. *(9 [10, 10, 11, 12] shells, 9 [10, 10, 11, 12] ch-2 sps)*

Rnd 9: Ch 2, sk next dc, (sc, ch 2, sc) in next dc, shell in next ch-2 sp, *(sc, ch 2, sc) in 3rd dc of next shell, shell in next ch-2 sp, rep from * around, join in beg sc. *(9 [10, 10, 11, 12] shells, 9 [10, 10, 11, 12] ch-2 sps)*

Rep rnds 8 and 9 alternately until piece measures 8½ [9, 9½, 10, 10½] inches from center of top, ending with rnd 9.

Edging

Sl st in first ch-2 sp, turn, ch 1, sc in same sp as beg ch-1, (sc, ch 2, sc) in first dc of next shell, [sk next dc, (sc, ch 2, sc) in next dc] twice, *sc in next ch-2 sp, (sc, ch 2, sc) in first dc of next shell, [sk next dc, (sc, ch 2, sc) in next dc] twice, rep from * around, join in beg sc. Fasten off. *(27 [30, 30, 33, 36] ch-2 sps, 9 [10, 10, 11, 12] sc)*

Fold Brim up to desired height.

Scarf

Size Toddler Only

Row 1: Ch 10, (sc, ch 2, sc) in 2nd ch from hook, sk next 3 chs, **shell** *(see Special Stitches)* in next ch, sk next 3 chs, (sc, ch 2, sc) in next ch, turn. *(2 ch-2 sps, 1 shell)*

Row 2: Sl st in first ch-2 sp, **beg shell** *(see Special Stitches)* in same sp, (sc, ch 2, sc) in 3rd dc of next shell, shell in next ch-2 sp, turn. *(1 ch-2 sp, 2 shells)*

Row 3: Ch 2, (sc, ch 2, sc) in 3rd dc of first shell, shell in next ch-2 sp, (sc, ch 2, sc) in 3rd dc of next shell, turn. *(2 ch-2 sps, 1 shell)*

Rep rows 2 and 3 alternately until piece measures 36 inches. At end of last row, fasten off.

Sizes Child, Tween, Woman & Man Only

Row [1]: Ch [18, 18, 26, 34], (sc, ch 2, sc) in 2nd ch from hook, *sk next 3 chs, **shell** *(see Special Stitches)* in next ch, sk next 3 chs, (sc, ch 2, sc) in next ch, rep from * across, turn. *([3, 3, 4, 5] ch-2 sps, [2, 2, 3, 4] shells)*

Row [2]: Sl st in first ch-2 sp, **beg shell** *(see Special Stitches)* in same sp, *(sc, ch 2, sc) in 3rd dc of next shell, shell in next ch-2 sp, rep from * across, turn. *([2, 2, 3, 4] ch-2 sps, [3, 3, 4, 5] shells)*

Row [3]: Ch 2, sk next dc, (sc, ch 2, sc) in next dc, *shell in next ch-2 sp, (sc, ch 2, sc) in 3rd dc of next shell, rep from * across, turn. *([3, 3, 4, 5] ch-2 sps, [2, 2, 3, 4] shells)*

Rep rows 2 and 3 alternately until piece measures [42, 48, 60, 72] inches.

At end of last row, fasten off.

Mitten
Make 2.

Rnd 1 (RS): Ch 7 [9, 9, 9, 11], 2 dc in 3rd ch from hook, dc in each of next 3 [5, 5, 5, 7] chs, 3 dc in last ch, working in unused lps on opposite side of foundation ch, dc in each of next 4 [6, 6, 6, 8] lps, **join** *(see Pattern Notes)* in 2nd ch of beg ch-2. *(12 [16, 16, 16, 20] dc)*

Rnd 2: Sl st in first dc, ch 1, (sc, ch 2, sc) in same dc, sk next dc, **half shell** *(see Special Stitches)* in next dc, sk next dc, [(sc, ch 2, sc) in next dc, sk next dc, half shell in next dc, sk next dc] 2 [3, 3, 3, 4] times, join in beg sc. *(3 [4, 4, 4, 5] half shells, 3 [4, 4, 4, 5] ch-2 sps)*

Rnd 3: Sl st in first ch-2 sp, **beg shell** *(see Special Stitches)* [**beg half shell** *(see Special Stitches)*, beg half shell, beg shell, beg shell] in same sp, (sc, ch 2, sc) in 2nd dc of next half shell, *shell *(see Special Stitches)* [half shell, half shell, shell, shell] in next ch-2 sp, (sc, ch 2, sc) in 2nd dc of next half shell, rep from * around, join in 3rd ch of beg ch-3. *(0 [4, 4, 0, 0] half shells, 3 [0, 0, 4, 5] shells, 3 [4, 4, 4, 5] ch-2 sps)*

Rnd 4: Ch 2 [1, 1, 2, 2], (sc, ch 2, sc) in center dc of first shell [half shell, half shell, shell, shell], shell [half shell, half shell, shell, shell] in next ch-2 sp, *(sc, ch 2, sc) in center dc of next shell [half shell, half shell, shell, shell], shell [half shell, half shell, shell, shell] in next ch-2 sp, rep from * around, join in beg sc. *(0 [4, 4, 0, 0] half shells, 3 [0, 0, 4, 5] shells, 3 [4, 4, 4, 5] ch-2 sps)*

Rnd 5: Sl st in first ch-2 sp, beg shell [beg half shell, beg half shell, beg shell, beg shell] in same sp, (sc, ch 2, sc) in center dc of next shell [half shell, half shell, shell, shell], *shell [half shell, half shell, shell, shell] in next ch-2 sp, (sc, ch 2, sc) in center dc of next shell [half shell, half shell, shell, shell], rep from * around, join in 3rd ch of beg ch-3. *(0 [4, 4, 0, 0] half shells, 3 [0, 0, 4, 5] shells, 3 [4, 4, 4, 5] ch-2 sps)*

Rep rnds 4 and 5 alternately until piece measures 3½ [4, 4½, 5½, 6½] inches from tip, ending with rnd 5.

Lower Hand

Rnd 1 (thumb opening): Sl st across to first ch-2 sp, beg shell [beg half shell, beg half shell, beg shell, beg shell] in same sp, *(sc, ch 2, sc) in center dc of next shell [half shell, half shell, shell, shell], shell [half shell, half shell, shell, shell] in next ch-2 sp, rep from * 1 [2, 2, 2, 3] time(s), ch 7, sk last shell [half shell, half shell, shell, shell], join in 3rd ch of beg ch-3. *(0 [4, 4, 0, 0] half shells, 3 [0, 0, 4, 5] shells, 2 [3, 3, 3, 4] ch-2 sps, 7 chs)*

Rnd 2: Ch 2 [1, 1, 2, 2], (sc, ch 2, sc) in center dc of first shell [half shell, half shell, shell, shell], *shell [half shell, half shell, shell, shell] in next ch-2 sp, (sc, ch 2, sc) in center dc of next shell [half shell, half shell, shell, shell], rep from * 1 [2, 2, 2, 3] time(s), half shell [half shell, half shell, shell, shell] in first ch, sk next 2 chs, (sc, ch 2, sc) in next ch, sk next 2 chs, half shell in last ch, join in beg sc. *(2 [5, 5, 1, 0] half shell(s), 2 [0, 0, 4, 6] shells, 4 [5, 5, 5, 6] ch-2 sps)*

Size Toddler Only

Rnd 3: Sl st in first ch-2 sp, beg shell in same sp, *(sc, ch 2, sc) in center dc of next shell, shell in next ch-2 sp, rep from * once, (sc, ch 2, sc) in center dc of next half shell, half shell in next ch-2 sp, (sc, ch 2, sc) in center dc of last half shell, join in 3rd ch of beg ch-3, turn. *(1 half shell, 3 shells, 4 ch-2 sps)*

Sizes Child, Tween, Woman & Man Only

Rnd [3]: Sl st in first ch-2 sp, [beg half shell, beg half shell, beg shell, beg shell] in same sp, *(sc, ch 2, sc)

in center dc of next [half shell, half shell, shell, shell], [half shell, half shell, shell, shell] in next ch-2 sp, rep from * around to last [half shell, half shell, shell, shell], (sc, ch 2, sc) in center dc of last [half shell, half shell, shell, shell], join in 3rd ch of beg ch-3, turn. *([5, 5, 0, 0] half shells, [0, 0, 5, 6] shells, [5, 5, 5, 6] ch-2 sps)*

Cuff

Rnd 1 (WS): Sl st in first ch-2 sp, ch 1, 4 [4, 4, 6, 5] hdc in same ch-2 sp as beg ch-1, sl st in center dc of next half shell [half shell, half shell, shell, shell], *4 [4, 4, 5, 5] hdc in next ch-2 sp, sl st in center dc of next shell [half shell, half shell, shell, shell], rep from * around, join in beg hdc, turn. *(16 [20, 20, 26, 30] hdc)*

Rnd 2 (RS): Ch 1, **fpdc** *(see Stitch Guide)* around first hdc, **bpdc** *(see Stitch Guide)* around next hdc, *fpdc around next hdc, bpdc around next hdc, rep from * around, leaving all sl sts unworked, join in beg fpdc. *(8 [10, 10, 13, 15] fpdc, 8 [10, 10, 13, 15] bpdc)*

Rnds 3 & 4 [3–5, 3–6, 3–7, 3–8]: Ch 1, fpdc around first st, bpdc around next st, *fpdc around next st, bpdc around next st, rep from * around, join in beg fpdc. At end of last rnd, fasten off. *(8 [10, 10, 13, 15] fpdc, 8 [10, 10, 13, 15] bpdc)*

Thumb

Note: *Thumb is worked in continuous rnds. Do not join unless specified; mark beg of rnds.*

Rnd 1: Hold piece with RS facing, join yarn in any st in thumb opening, ch 1, working in sts around thumb opening, work 11 [13, 13, 15, 17] sc evenly sp around. *(11 [13, 13, 15, 17] sc)*

Rnd 2: Sc in each sc around.

Rep rnd 2 until piece measures ½ [¾, ¾, 1, 1¼] inch(es) from rnd 1.

Note: *On following rnds, do not use same sts for dec on each rnd; sp dec apart.*

Continue to work in continuous rnds, working 1 **sc dec** *(see Stitch Guide)* in 2 sts of each rnd until piece measures 1¾ [2, 2¼, 2¾, 3] inches from rnd 1.

At end of last rnd, join in first sc. Fasten off, leaving 12-inch end for sewing.

Finishing

Turn Mittens inside out and weave yarn through sts of last rnd, pull end to close. Secure end. ●

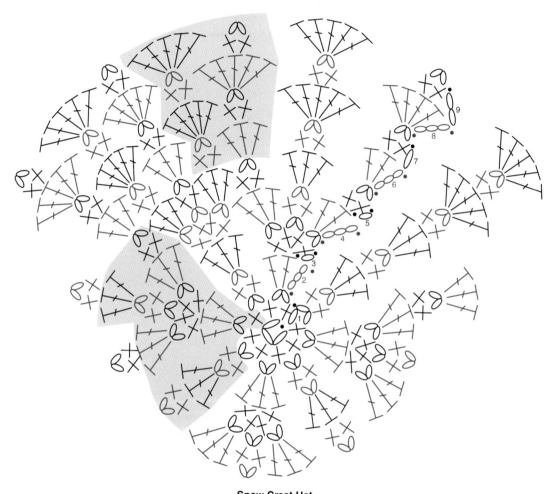

Snow Crest Hat
Size Toddler Stitch Diagram
Note: Reps shown in gray.

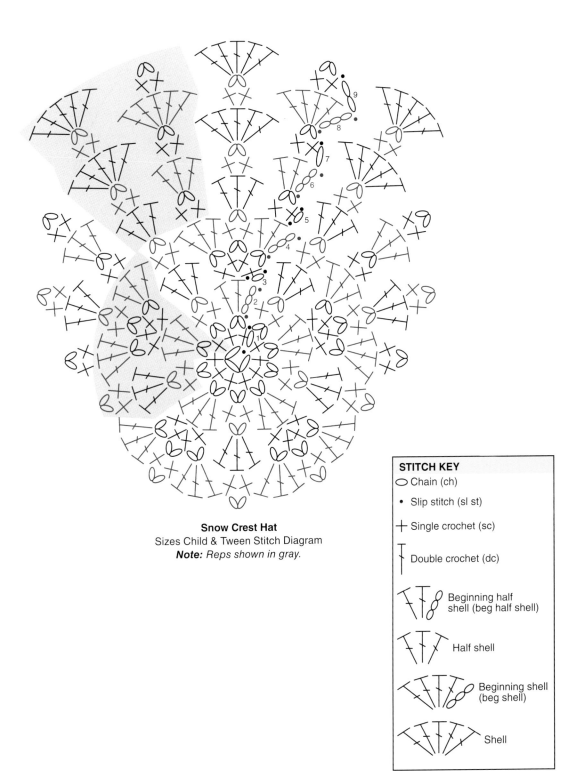

Snow Crest Hat
Sizes Child & Tween Stitch Diagram
Note: Reps shown in gray.

STITCH KEY

⌒ Chain (ch)

• Slip stitch (sl st)

+ Single crochet (sc)

┬ Double crochet (dc)

Beginning half shell (beg half shell)

Half shell

Beginning shell (beg shell)

Shell

Snow Crest Hat
Size Woman Stitch Diagram
Note: *Reps shown in gray.*

Snow Crest Hat
Size Man Stitch Diagram
Note: Reps shown in gray.

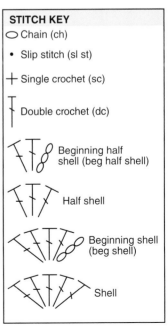

STITCH KEY

◯ Chain (ch)

• Slip stitch (sl st)

+ Single crochet (sc)

┬ Double crochet (dc)

Beginning half shell (beg half shell)

Half shell

Beginning shell (beg shell)

Shell

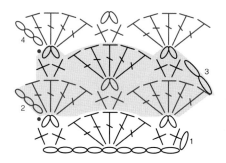

Snow Crest
Size Toddler Scarf Stitch Diagram
Note: Reps shown in gray.

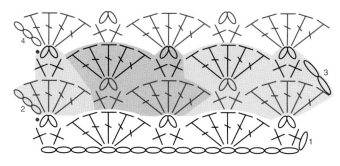

Snow Crest
Sizes Child, Tween, Woman & Man Scarf Stitch Diagram
Note: Reps shown in gray.

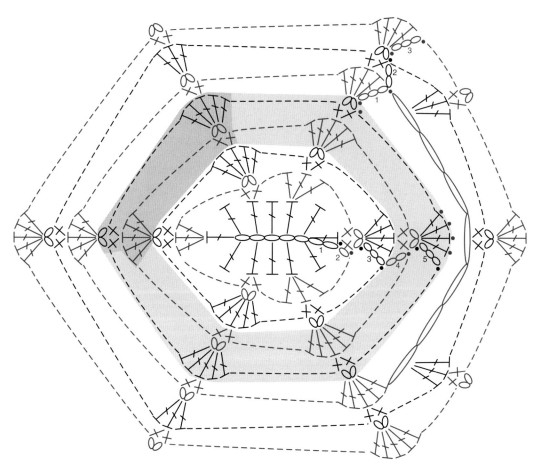

Snow Crest
Size Toddler Mitten Stitch Diagram
Note: Reps shown in gray.

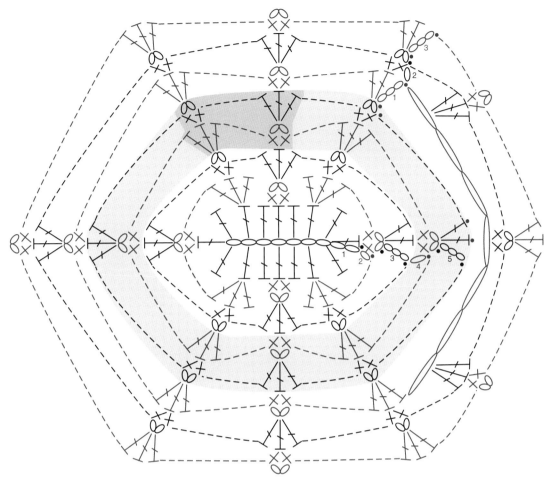

Snow Crest
Sizes Child and Tween Mitten Stitch Diagram
Note: *Reps shown in gray.*

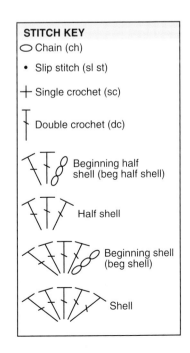

STITCH KEY

⬯ Chain (ch)

• Slip stitch (sl st)

+ Single crochet (sc)

⊤ Double crochet (dc)

Beginning half shell (beg half shell)

Half shell

Beginning shell (beg shell)

Shell

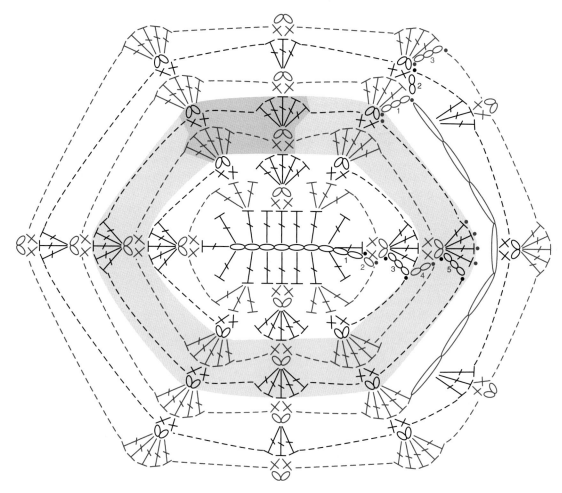

Snow Crest
Size Woman Mitten Stitch Diagram
Note: *Reps shown in gray.*

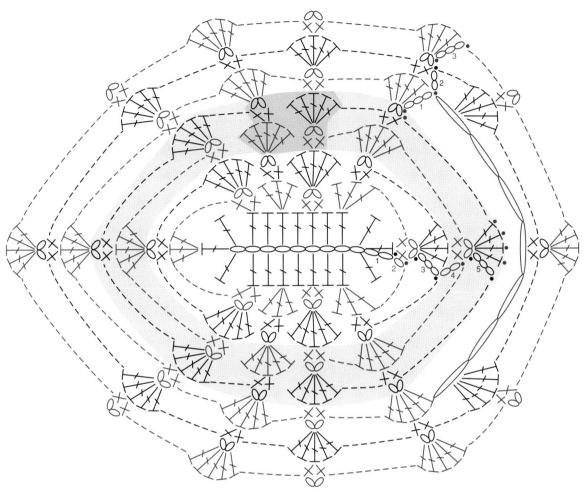

Snow Crest
Size Man Mitten Stitch Diagram
Note: *Reps shown in gray.*

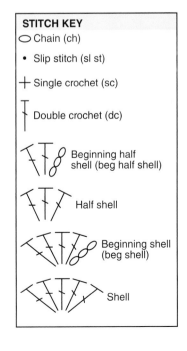

STITCH KEY

⬭ Chain (ch)

• Slip stitch (sl st)

+ Single crochet (sc)

† Double crochet (dc)

Beginning half shell (beg half shell)

Half shell

Beginning shell (beg shell)

Shell

Metric Conversion Charts

METRIC CONVERSIONS

yards	x	.9144	=	metres (m)
yards	x	91.44	=	centimetres (cm)
inches	x	2.54	=	centimetres (cm)
inches	x	25.40	=	millimetres (mm)
inches	x	.0254	=	metres (m)

centimetres	x	.3937	=	inches
metres	x	1.0936	=	yards

INCHES INTO MILLIMETRES & CENTIMETRES (Rounded off slightly)

inches	mm	cm	inches	cm	inches	cm	inches	cm
1/8	3	0.3	5	12.5	21	53.5	38	96.5
1/4	6	0.6	5 1/2	14	22	56	39	99
3/8	10	1	6	15	23	58.5	40	101.5
1/2	13	1.3	7	18	24	61	41	104
5/8	15	1.5	8	20.5	25	63.5	42	106.5
3/4	20	2	9	23	26	66	43	109
7/8	22	2.2	10	25.5	27	68.5	44	112
1	25	2.5	11	28	28	71	45	114.5
1 1/4	32	3.2	12	30.5	29	73.5	46	117
1 1/2	38	3.8	13	33	30	76	47	119.5
1 3/4	45	4.5	14	35.5	31	79	48	122
2	50	5	15	38	32	81.5	49	124.5
2 1/2	65	6.5	16	40.5	33	84	50	127
3	75	7.5	17	43	34	86.5		
3 1/2	90	9	18	46	35	89		
4	100	10	19	48.5	36	91.5		
4 1/2	115	11.5	20	51	37	94		

KNITTING NEEDLES CONVERSION CHART

Canada/U.S.	0	1	2	3	4	5	6	7	8	9	10	10½	11	13	15
Metric (mm)	2	2¼	2¾	3¼	3½	3¾	4	4½	5	5½	6	6½	8	9	10

CROCHET HOOKS CONVERSION CHART

Canada/U.S.	1/B	2/C	3/D	4/E	5/F	6/G	8/H	9/I	10/J	10½/K	N
Metric (mm)	2.25	2.75	3.25	3.5	3.75	4.25	5	5.5	6	6.5	9.0

STITCH GUIDE

STITCH ABBREVIATIONS

beg . . . . begin/begins/beginning
bpdc . . . . back post double crochet
bpsc . . . . .back post single crochet
bptr. . . . . .back post treble crochet
CC. . . . . contrasting color
ch(s) . . . . .chain(s)
ch- . . . . refers to chain or space previously made (i.e., ch-1 space)
ch sp(s) . . . . chain space(s)
cl(s) . . . . cluster(s)
cm . . . . centimeter(s)
dc. . . . . double crochet (singular/plural)
dc dec. double crochet 2 or more stitches together, as indicated
dec. decrease/decreases/decreasing
dtr . . . . double treble crochet
ext . . . . .extended
fpdc. . . . . front post double crochet
fpsc . . . . front post single crochet
fptr . . . . front post treble crochet
g . . . . gram(s)
hdc . . . . half double crochet
hdc dec . . . . half double crochet 2 or more stitches together, as indicated
inc . . . . increase/increases/increasing
lp(s) . . . . .loop(s)
MC . . . . .main color
mm . . . . .millimeter(s)
oz . . . . .ounce(s)
pc . . . . popcorn(s)
rem . . . . .remain/remains/remaining
rep(s) . . . . .repeat(s)
rnd(s) . . . . round(s)
RS . . . . .right side
sc . . . . single crochet (singular/plural)
sc dec . . . . single crochet 2 or more stitches together, as indicated
sk . . . . .skip/skipped/skipping
sl st(s) . . . . slip stitch(es)
sp(s) . . . . space(s)/spaced
st(s) . . . . stitch(es)
tog. . . . . .together
tr. . . . . treble crochet
trtr. . . . . .triple treble
WS . . . . wrong side
yd(s) . . . . .yard(s)
yo . . . . yarn over

YARN CONVERSION

OUNCES TO GRAMS		GRAMS TO OUNCES	
1	28.4	25	⅞
2	56.7	40	1⅔
3	85.0	50	1¾
4	113.4	100	3½

UNITED STATES		UNITED KINGDOM
sl st (slip stitch)	=	sc (single crochet)
sc (single crochet)	=	dc (double crochet)
hdc (half double crochet)	=	htr (half treble crochet)
dc (double crochet)	=	tr (treble crochet)
tr (treble crochet)	=	dtr (double treble crochet)
dtr (double treble crochet)	=	ttr (triple treble crochet)
skip	=	miss

Single crochet decrease (sc dec): (Insert hook, yo, draw lp through) in each of the sts indicated, yo, draw through all lps on hook.

Example of 2-sc dec

Half double crochet decrease (hdc dec): (Yo, insert hook, yo, draw lp through) in each of the sts indicated, yo, draw through all lps on hook.

Example of 2-hdc dec

Reverse single crochet (reverse sc): Ch 1, sk first st, working from left to right, insert hook in next st from front to back, draw up lp on hook, yo and draw through both lps on hook.

Chain (ch): Yo, pull through lp on hook.

Single crochet (sc): Insert hook in st, yo, pull through st, yo, pull through both lps on hook.

Double crochet (dc): Yo, insert hook in st, yo, pull through st, [yo, pull through 2 lps] twice.

Double crochet decrease (dc dec): (Yo, insert hook, yo, draw lp through, yo, draw through 2 lps on hook) in each of the sts indicated, yo, draw through all lps on hook.

Example of 2-dc dec

Front loop (front lp) Back loop (back lp)

Front Loop   Back Loop

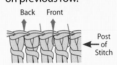

Front post stitch (fp): Back post stitch (bp): When working post st, insert hook from right to left around post of st on previous row.

Back   Front

Post of Stitch

Half double crochet (hdc): Yo, insert hook in st, yo, pull through st, yo, pull through all 3 lps on hook.

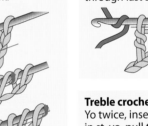

Double treble crochet (dtr): Yo 3 times, insert hook in st, yo, pull through st, [yo, pull through 2 lps] 4 times.

Treble crochet decrease (tr dec): Holding back last lp of each st, tr in each of the sts indicated, yo, pull through all lps on hook.

Example of 2-tr dec

Slip stitch (sl st): Insert hook in st, pull through both lps on hook.

Chain color change (ch color change) Yo with new color, draw through last lp on hook.

Double crochet color change (dc color change) Drop first color, yo with new color, draw through last 2 lps of st.

Treble crochet (tr): Yo twice, insert hook in st, yo, pull through st, [yo, pull through 2 lps] 3 times.

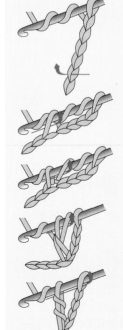

Stylishly Warm Hats & Scarves is published by Annie's, 306 East Parr Road, Berne, IN 46711. Printed in USA. Copyright © 2015 Annie's. All rights reserved. This publication may not be reproduced in part or in whole without written permission from the publisher.

RETAIL STORES: If you would like to carry this publication or any other Annie's publication, visit AnniesWSL.com.

Every effort has been made to ensure that the instructions in this publication are complete and accurate. We cannot, however, take responsibility for human error, typographical mistakes or variations in individual work. Please visit AnniesCustomerService.com to check for pattern updates.

ISBN: 978-1-57367-945-9

1 2 3 4 5 6 7 8 9